OWN
YOUR
PASSION

BY
JASAUN MONCRIEF

Library of Congress Cataloging-in-Publication Data

Jasaun Moncrief
Own Your Passion: Turn Your Idea into A Successful Business
Published by: Adam Divine Publishing, LLC

ISBN: 978-1-7325335-0-9
10 9 8 7 6 5 4 3 2 1
Printed in the United States of America

Note: This book is intended only as a real-life testimony of the life and wisdom of Jasaun Moncrief. Readers are advised to consult a professional before making any changes in their life. The reader assumes all responsibility for the consequences of any actions taken based on the information presented in this book. The information in this book is based on the author's research and experience. Every attempt has been made to ensure that the information is accurate; however, the author cannot accept liability for any errors that may exist. The facts and theories about life are subject to interpretation, and the conclusions and recommendations presented here may not agree with other interpretations.

TABLE OF CONTENTS

INTRODUCTION

Do you have a burning desire to start a business doing something you love? One definition of passion is "a strong liking or desire for a particular activity, object, or concept," such as a passion for playing chess. I can remember the scene of this turning point in my life like it was yesterday. I was at a local Starbucks coffee shop studying the Bible in some capacity. Perhaps I was completing a seminary school assignment, preparing for a sermon, or simply enjoying reading the Word of God. I felt a great deal of gratitude and appreciation for how far I had come in life, but it still felt like something was missing. This nagging feeling began to stir up my emotions like never before. So, I did what any man/woman of faith should do. I began to pray and ask God for clarification. I asked him to reveal to me this missing piece. The missing piece was a passion for entrepreneurship, which includes implementing and teaching fundamentally-sound business principles. Learning about what it takes to create and maintain a successful business venture has always piqued my interest. I was intrigued by the stories of those who overcame major obstacles to become successful. The commonalities I found were that they enjoyed learning, took calculated risks, displayed courage, and in the end, were able to help their families and others by providing a demand for a product or service. This curiosity is the reason that I pursued and obtained my Bachelor's degree in Business Management; my road to becoming a legitimate business owner began and ended in divine fashion.

Caught up in the moment, I entertained the thought of starting my own clothing line. There were moments of doubt, when I presumed that a clothing line might be too trendy. After all, my intent was not to follow trends. However, the thought of starting my own clothing line persisted in my mind and the thought was somewhat powerful.

Over the years, I have learned valuable lessons regarding spiritual confirmation. One lesson I learned is recognizing the presence of peace involved when God is the one providing direction. In other words, there is no confusion present. This is what I felt in that moment.

So, I remember telling myself that my clothing line will be original and managed using Godly principles. I began searching for words that represented originality and divinity. I came up with "Adam," since he was biblically referred to as the original man, and "Divine," which means "of God." I had a name for my clothing line. I thought to myself, *"Adam Divine." Yeah, I like the sound of that.* I could see Adam Divine being mentioned in the same breath with the likes of True Religion or Christian Dior. The name not only had a good feel and sound, but it also was created with purpose and power. My next step was to create a logo, so I searched the internet for some related images. My plan was to find an image or symbol that both caught my eye and somehow related to the name Adam Divine. I visualized wings with the letters "AD" in special font. I visualized the letters within a circle located in the middle of the wings. This whole process took less than an hour. I was amazed that the vision was so clear and came to me so quickly. Once I finalized the name and visual for the logo, I shut down my computer and headed right over to Arrow Printing. Arrow Printing is a local print shop that I used in the past for flyers and business cards. Arrow Printing has become a very important aspect of the Adam Divine team. Within a few days, they sent me a digital copy of the new logo. I registered the clothing as an LLC and officially trademarked the logo. To sum it all up, giving all glory to God, I decided to own my passion.

CHAPTER 1
The Perfect Marriage

The road to entrepreneurship has served as a tremendous blessing in my life. When I wake up in the morning, there is excitement where there previously was none. I thank God for the blessing to have a business based on passion and purpose. To have multiple platforms bringing my creative ideas to life is an indescribable feeling. When someone is speaking about their area of passion, you can hear it in their voice. The energy becomes visually evident. Around my hometown, people often will approach me and offer to support my businesses. Many times, the support comes from a person I haven't seen in years; the opportunities to connect and reconnect are truly inspirational.

Owning your passion is a rewarding experience. To be continually engaged in something you love to do is beneficial to your life on many different levels. Everyone should invest time in their interests and talents, even if it's just engaging in your passion as a hobby or side project. However, on a business level, you will generate your best results by integrating your passion with a specific skill. For example, I have a passion for entrepreneurship, and I've been told that I'm moderately skillful as a writer and speaker. Writing and speaking are not necessarily passions of mine, but entrepreneurship is. So, what opportunities could be birthed from combining my passion with a specific skill? A couple of years ago, I found an old English textbook from my college days. I graduated with a degree in Business Management from Alabama State University, and like most undergraduates, I had to take a general course or two in English. Finding this book turned out to be a blessing; it sparked an idea that helped propel me on my business journey. This book covered everything from formulating sentences to writing business reports. I had the foresight to know that, whether it was ascending the corporate ladder or launching my own business, writing would be a valuable skill to help me succeed. I used search engines to identify the most important skills to have in relation to achieving success. I began to notice a pattern; writing and speaking were necessary tools across all avenues of success. I had an epiphany; developing my writing skills would prove to be beneficial in whatever future path I chose. I decided to pursue a second degree in English or obtain a professional writing certificate. Once I formed a list of schools with reputable writing programs, I went online and completed several applications. Driving home from work one day, I received a phone call from one of the prospective universities to which I applied. At this point, I was not totally committed to actually starting the process of becoming a student. My plate was full of my responsibilities as a minister, father, and insurance agent. However, something felt different about this phone call. As the enrollment specialist explained the final application process, my inner voice advised me to be patient and listen. Now, I work about an hour away from home, and before I made the full commute, we had already laid most of the groundwork needed to initiate my status as a college student again. I was excited and nervous at the same time, but I also know that God works in mysterious ways. Some things just instinctively feel good in your spirit.

After completing the preliminary administrative tasks, I began the journey of attaining a second degree in English. These were online classes, so it was fast-paced and quite different from the methods of the past. Again, I admit I was a little bit nervous about enrolling in school while still taking care of life's other responsibilities. Managing my time properly was imperative to ensure my academic success. The university did provide a mandatory preparation class; this was beneficial in helping me to become acclimated to the online academic process. One of my first classes was English Literature. Each student was required to provide weekly posts to receive a passing grade. A weekly essay was assigned based on specific topics chosen by the instructor. It was a lot of work, but once I learned how to balance school with my personal life, I began to enjoy the rush of the workload. I really began to enjoy posting and reading the other students' work. A specific number of posts had to be completed, but credit could be earned for creating posts and responding to other students. The instructor read our posts and gave credit when the posting requirements were met. The credit was contingent on a post's relevancy, length and level of articulation. Beneath each post, the instructor responded and commented. I realized that I was receiving positive comments on most of my posts. At the end of the week, we had to complete an essay along with other assignments. That first week was arduous; I remember still being awake around 1:30 am, completing the essay assignment. At the beginning of the week, all assignments were graded, giving us access to updated, accumulated grades. After that nerve-wrecking first week of being back in college, I finished the week with an A. These accelerated classes only lasted for four weeks, so getting off to a great start was very important. I could feel my confidence growing and building tremendously, and I started to look forward to completing the writing assignments. Those four weeks flew by and my final class grade was excellent. The professor complimented my written work and called me "a great asset to the class." With my writing confidence gaining momentum, along with improved time management skills, I was highly anticipating my next writing class. English 101 was the next class and, of course, it consisted of a ton of writing assignments. As soon as the class began, I started completing my assignments as quickly as possible. I posted way above the minimum weekly requirements. My intention was not to show off, but along with being more confident as a writer, I felt I had a lot to share on the chosen topics. Based on the way the instructor and students responded to my work, I could see early on that I was viewed as a leader.

Although writing was not a passion of mine, I was beginning to somewhat enjoy it. More than the writing itself, I relished the process of researching topics and sharing my thoughts about information I discovered. I had always enjoyed reading, and I quickly learned that writing served as an avenue for me to express what I read and learned. During this time, I continued to develop marketing and operations for my clothing line. At the same time, I created a blog to write about business-related topics. It was not simply a hobby; the purpose of the blog was to help market my products and inspire other entrepreneurs to own their passion. From my blogging efforts, I received quality feedback leading to free marketing and additional sales. I begin to reap the benefits of writing from a personal and business standpoint. Simultaneously, I developed my writing skills, and utilized them to engage in my passion of entrepreneurship. All of these efforts fulfilled an untapped part of me, preparing me to receive news that would confirm I was traveling down the right path. It was also an indication of how there will be times when you must rely on your instincts, if the desire is to be successful and achieve extraordinary results. Similar to the previous class, the required four weeks flew by extremely fast. At the end of the last week of class, I turned in my final essay and we all were waiting to receive our final grade. I anticipated earning either an A- or B+ depending on the quality of my final essay. I was really focused on maintaining a 4.0 grade point average, so receiving a B would have been a disappointment. It seemed that the teacher was a little behind schedule with posting grades, so I decided to contact him personally. When I spoke with him, I could immediately sense his passion for teaching and his abundance of wisdom. He advised me that the grades would be posted later that same day or the following day. His next revelation took me by surprise and served as more confirmation that I was on the right path. He told me I was one of the most gifted students he encountered throughout his entire teaching career, both in academics and the corporate arena. This confidence booster was extra motivation to proactively use my writing skills in the business arena. So, whether it be writing business developmental books, blogging, or creating marketing ads, writing has increased my passion for business. The skill you choose may not be writing but combining your passion with a critical skill will help you become more effective as an entrepreneur. It is one of the essential building blocks to truly owning your passion.

CHAPTER 2
Smile & Serve

Managing your business in an effective way is essential to becoming a profitable company. Being profitable in business should be one of your main goals, but it should not be the only goal. At some point, a business should serve a purpose that reaches beyond revenue and contributes to the well-being of others. Some business owner's focus on this aspect in the launching stages, and others gradually shift to this stage as their businesses progress and expand. Operating your business with a purpose means to intentionally focus on helping others through your business endeavors. I'm very grateful that my business allows me to support my family and simultaneously contribute to helping others become successful. Adam Divine Business Coaching allows me to help business owners build something that can change their lives in multiple ways. It also allows me to reach back into my community in a charitable way, by helping and encouraging burgeoning entrepreneurs to cultivate the skills necessary for success. Aside from spiritual salvation, economic development in urban communities should be a major focus for those in leadership positions. My two areas of passion are the Word of God and entrepreneurship. My professional coaching business allows me to share my testimony while assisting clients in formulating and completing a very thorough business plan. We also show clients how to constantly review and revise their plans, which helps their business to grow. I am confident that my business is operating with a deliberate and powerful purpose.

Recently, I met with a client who was struggling to create a business plan. She understood the importance of having a business plan, but like most new business owners, she was not completely clear on how to put one together herself. She desperately needed some professional assistance. During the first business coaching session, I like to learn about my clients personally and get an understanding of why they decided to become entrepreneurs. At our first meeting, clients generally display a true passion and purpose for starting their own business. The fire is there. They begin to tell stories of hardship, and how they overcame numerous obstacles before getting started. When I sense the joy inside them as they share their stories of perseverance and determination, I immediately encourage them to continue to move forward and fully own their passion. I congratulate them for taking the initial step and advise them that faith, hard work, and perseverance will take them to enormous heights. Knowing that my services can help empower those who seek me as a business coach inspires me as well. I would encourage all business owners to not only learn how to operate a profitable business, but also to diligently find a deeper purpose for transforming your passion into profit. As an entrepreneur, never forget to ask yourself how your product and service can help contribute to the well-being of others. This will help you move with purpose, which in the end, will be much more fulfilling than just moving for a profit. Like myself, many of my clients view their new businesses as gifts from God that will help them build something valuable for themselves and others. I enjoy listening to new business owners explain to me why they decided to take the leap into becoming business owners. I patiently listen to their stories, usually filled with excitement, anxiousness, confusion and often times, fear. I know those feelings well. I can relate because I was once in their shoes. My business was, and still is, a gift from God because it's part of my overall purpose. With every client I've assisted, there has been an opportunity for me to share my testimony. My testimony describes how my faith in God allowed me to bounce back from extremely hard times. Then I explain to them how God blessed me with a business founded on purpose and passion. Some people choose to separate their faith and business. I openly express my desire for God to be the foundation of everything I develop, both personally and professionally. My aim is to continuously serve my customers to the best of my ability. As a business owner, serving your clients should not be simply a task; it should be considered a pleasure. When you reach a point where you truly enjoy serving your customers to the best of your ability, profits will soon follow in abundance.

CHAPTER 3
They Think You're Amazing

One of the greatest aspects of following your dreams and becoming an entrepreneur is your inevitable ability to inspire others. When I explain how I took something I was passionate about and transformed it into a legitimate business, it amazes people. I still get inspired myself when I witness an entrepreneur conducting business with a passion.

When a "foodie," someone who truly loves food, opens a restaurant, it's almost guaranteed that the food will be above average. When you encounter a mechanic, who loves everything about vehicles, you can sense the passion as he explains to you what he's about to repair. I love to tell my story and watch it light a fire in other people.

One story that inspired me was the story of Ralph Lauren. I once watched a documentary about how he started from very humble beginnings. Ralph Lauren started off selling neckties and then graduated to producing other clothing items. The story displayed how he truly believed in his brand from the beginning, which was evident when his vision came to fruition and he began negotiating with major retail stores. The longevity of the Ralph Lauren brand is astounding; how his company managed to stay relevant for so long can be an inspiration to any entrepreneur. The Ralph Lauren brand has transcended generations. I remember wearing his polo shirts when I was in high school, and to see my son wearing the same polo shirts is absolutely astounding to me. One thing I have learned about business is that high quality never goes out of style. We all should find people or stories that provide us with inspiration; knowing the success of others can help to keep you inspired and motivated.

One of the most amazing business people I ever met was my Grandmother Carrie Henderson. She was an educated woman, but following her retirement from the school system, she began to invest in real estate. She was very organized and passionate about her business. She ended up owning multiple real estate properties in our local area. She purchased the properties at low or reasonable prices and then rented them out to the locals for profit. She was skilled at taking properties that needed to be rehabilitated and rejuvenating them into renovated homes at affordable rental rates. Many times, I returned home from college and drove her around to look at potential properties she was considering for purchase. Occasionally, she would ask for my opinion before she made the purchase. When it came to purchasing the properties, she had established a great business relationship with a wealthy businessman who had his own finance company. This businessman was known for purchasing multiple properties at once. This also was one of the first times I witnessed the importance of developing good business relationships. Forming good relationships can help expedite your success and shorten the learning curve. This specific business relationship led to my grandmother's access to a large supply of potential rental properties she could purchase at her convenience. Her business partner knew she was reliable and possessed the ability to capitalize on every investment.

Their relationship was built on trust and integrity. My grandmother hired local handymen who were paid competitive wages to maintain the rental properties. Their backgrounds did not matter; if she trusted them and they performed quality work, she employed them. I now realize that her business was used as a ministry of love. She developed positive relationships with these workers and served as a mother figure to them in many ways. Witnessing our family benefit from the income she generated from these rental properties, watching her provide the less fortunate with consistent work, and seeing the sincere business relationships she developed makes her one of my business heroes. My grandmother is now deceased but watching her rise to success as an entrepreneur is still a great source of inspiration for me. As an entrepreneur, strive for excellence; you never know who is watching and learning from you. As you begin to own your passion, there is someone out there watching who thinks you're absolutely amazing. As leaders and entrepreneurs, we have the responsibility to always do our absolute best. This will set an example of excellence that will pass down from generation to generation.

CHAPTER 4
Admit That You Are in Love

When you realize you have a true passion about something, never let fear stop you from taking it to the next level. One thing that saddens me most is when people allow fear to stop them from pursuing their dreams. Other than my relationship with God, and the birth of my children, the thing I am most proud of is creating a legitimate business around my passion. I truly thank God for answering my prayers and giving me the vision and courage to start my own business. I understood that stepping out and trying something completely new was risky. I understood how most people probably thought I would fail and give up on my dream after a short period of time. I also knew a lot of people would unjustly criticize my ideas and not show support for my business endeavors. These thoughts briefly ran through my head in the beginning phase, but fear did not stop me because I had a true passion for entrepreneurship. People may be unable to see your vision in the beginning, but once success starts to manifest, and you create a quality product, the support will follow. I truly believe part of being original is fully embracing who you are and being comfortable in your own skin.

Looking over my life in retrospect and regretting not following my dreams would have been one of my worst nightmares. Opportunities will come and go quickly if procrastination persists. If you have a desire to provide the world with a quality product or service, immediately take the first step required to own your passion. Practice embracing who you truly are by performing courageous acts every day until being fearless becomes a habit. Talk and walk like the successful entrepreneur that you are. Visualize yourself living a successful life every day, living out your passion and using your God-given abilities to serve others. The irony is that once you have overcome obstacles and barriers, the very people who doubted and criticized you may end up being inspired by your acts of courage. Being a successful businessperson does require planning and skill, but having a fearless attitude is of the utmost importance.

Embracing your passion is imperative, because typically, your passion is an essential part of who you are. Remember, the word "passion" refers to healthy things you love - things that are fulfilling, productive and beneficial to others. I once read a book titled *Emotional Intelligence 2.0* by Travis Bradberry & Jean Greaves. This book had a positive impact on my growth as both a leader and businessman. Learning how to be self-aware was one of the areas that most benefited me. The self- awareness section in the book provides strategies that help individuals become more aware of traits that make up their personality. Learning about your true self on this level gives you the ability to recognize and understand your emotions. This skill is important to be able to respond to those emotions effectively. I recognized and began to embrace my desire to research and study for long periods of time. I appreciated my own thirst for knowledge. In the industry of building businesses, it's almost like I transform into a scientist who likes to spend long hours in the lab. During these times, I prefer to be alone, away from all distractions. I do realize this is somewhat of an introverted personality trait. However, I recognized my ability to produce my best work in this zone. Not only do I understand this personality trait, I have embraced it. Adam Divine Clothing was birthed from this particular emotion or behavior, as some would call it. Once the idea popped in my head, and I viewed it as more than just a fantasy, I literally became a scientist and locked myself in the lab. Every day for two months, I researched clothing materials, distribution channels, business technology, best practices etc. I did not chat on the phone or watch television because I was completely focused on owning my passion.

As a former college athlete, I enjoy watching sports, but during the time I was building my business, I didn't even have a desire to tune in to any games. I was extremely focused on completing this project. When you become self-aware and embrace your true self, it allows you to reflect over your life. Certain things begin to make sense. For example, in my last year of college, like most students, my entire focus was aimed at earning my degree. One of my closest friends was in the midst of earning his Bachelor's degree in accounting. He was extremely dedicated and possessed some of the best study habits I ever witnessed. I used to watch him stay up all night studying, take a quick nap and then finish studying until it was time for his morning class. I was all for maintaining good study habits, but I thought this practice was a little extreme. We all need our rest, right? However, I witnessed the results of his hard work and watched my friend graduate with honors. I took a page from his playbook and began to develop this same practice; "I started to enjoy what I call subject matter mastery." We enrolled in a couple of classes together and adopted a phrase for this mode of studying. We labeled this method of long studying "pulling all-nighters." We would start studying early in the day, take a quick nap and continue studying until class began in the morning on test day. It seems we never earned less than 95 – 100% on those tests. This is when I started to embrace what I call my "inner nerd," developing a real success mind state. Researching and studying for extremely long periods of time started to become second nature. I believe I am still benefiting from those experiences today. I can study scripture for hours at a time, or research new business concepts at length because of this habit I developed in college. It is now part of who I am, and this habit has helped me reach heights that didn't seem possible before. As a new business owner, learn to embrace those productive – even if peculiar - traits you possess. Continue to be original and embrace the fact that God has designed you like no one else.

CHAPTER 5
Make It Official

This is where you take your passion and legally turn it into an official business. Just because a person is conducting business doesn't make them legitimate in the eyes of the government. Also, failing to have your business properly registered with your local and state government, you run the risk of missing out on potential benefits for business owners.

When I refer to "owning your passion," it refers to spiritually, mentally, emotionally, and legally maintaining it. The legal aspect is very important, because it is an avenue for you to elevate your business to another level and provides opportunity to attract higher-level clientele. Many of us are aware of people who are very talented at their craft, but they conduct business in an underground fashion without ever legitimizing their business. This is more prevalent in the inner city. The misconception is that registering a business is difficult -this is a myth. Registering your business is a very simple process. The foremost decision to be made is whether you want to register your business as a DBA, LLC,

C or S Corp etc. It is commonplace for start-up companies to register as an LLC (Limited Liability Corporation) because of the simplicity of registration coupled with many of the same benefits of a large corporation. However, every situation is different. These options should be thoroughly researched to make a decision that best fits your individual situation. Once you decide on this structure, registering the business is fairly simple. The entire process can be completed in matter of a few days in most states. The process may only consist of filling out one simple form, then faxing/emailing that to your state business division. For legal requirements and growth opportunities, registering your business properly is mandatory. Also, in order to open a business bank account, you must have a Federal Tax ID number for the business. You can only receive the federal tax ID number after you have registered the business properly on the local/state level. Once I received my confirmation from the state, I was able to provide my business information to the federal government and obtain my Federal Tax ID instantly. All of this was possible online. The next step was to choose a local bank to open a business checking account. Shortly after, I received my debit cards in the mail, and everything was legally ready to go. Once you have opened a bank account for your business, you will be authorized to write and receive checks. Most people may think writing checks is a thing of the past. However, some high-level clients will prefer to write you a check to pay for your services. You want to be able to deposit and cash that check in a timely manner without paying additional and unnecessary fees. The entire registration process should take no more than a few days or a week at best if you familiarize yourself with the steps. Don't hesitate to consult a business coach to assist you with this registration process if necessary. By no means should you allow this simple process to intimidate you and stop you from legally owning your passion. Plus, if you decide you want to start applying for loans, the business will need to be properly registered.

Another benefit of having your business registered properly is receiving tax breaks. Things such as gas expenses, phone expenses, computer purchases, business dinners, can all possibly be written off as business expenses at the end of year. Research and check with your accountant or tax professional to get a better understanding of these tax benefits. I encourage you as an entrepreneur to conduct your business the proper way to enjoy the many benefits of becoming a business owner.

CHAPTER 6
Travel with A Map

Creating a business plan is a fundamental part of becoming a business owner. Once you complete your business plan, it should become a living document. The plan is not made to be put on a shelf. The plan should be used as a tool that is consistently reviewed and revised. This will help you to continuously improve your business and attain the results you desire. It's all about business planning - not just creating a business plan. To achieve success in business, a great starting point is to understand the components of a thorough business plan. Otherwise, how can you improve something you don't really comprehend? One method of creating a business plan is the format used by Live Plan (Palo Alto). Identifying the main problem to be solved is a logical place to start when completing your business plan. Many new business owners struggle to create a strong business plan. Additionally, most business owners eventually recognize that they need to have a business plan to get any type of funding. However, a lot of them don't realize the importance of having a business plan for internal direction. A good business plan is a roadmap that will help guide you toward your destination. It will help you determine what's working and what's not. It will help you overcome being "stuck." I started Adam Divine Business Coaching with the understanding that a lot of business owners felt overwhelmed by the process of creating a business plan. I quickly identified this as a major problem for new business owners in my area. The most successful businesses in the world are those that identify a problem and solve it in a way that is better than their competitors. When you strip a business down to the core purpose it's really that simple; so, start your business identifying a problem you are passionate about solving and commit to solving that problem better than your competitors. Business coaching is a very broad discipline involving many different facets. It can include components such as mentoring, goal setting, sales training, financial projections, budgeting etc.

I knew I would eventually become a business coach, but I didn't know which area of coaching would become my specialty. After pondering over this situation, I asked myself an important question: What do new business owners really need? The answer is that they need to create and understand every component of a business plan. This will guide them internally and help them receive funding from banks and investors. A complete business plan contains multiple components, so this would require additional work on my end. Even though it would require more work, my gut told me this service would serve a major need in my local business community. I completed the steps required to become a certified business coach. Becoming certified in a discipline I was passionate about was a major accomplishment for me. I highly encourage you to further your education around your God-given gifts and passions. You will reap tremendous blessings by doing this. After I completed the business coaching certification, I registered the business with my state. Shortly after, I posted my services on a couple of social media sites. Almost instantly, I received offers to conduct individual coaching sessions and host a business planning workshop. I felt blessed for the opportunity and somewhat amazed how quickly things begin to unfold. Why did my business begin to take off so quickly? I believe it was because of two things: I serve an awesome God, and my business services provided a real solution to a common problem. Remember to ensure that your business serves a legitimate need, and you won't have to worry about attracting customers. Now learning how to retain these customers is the subject of another topic. For now, simply identify and focus on the problem your business will solve.

CHAPTER 7
They Need Your Help!

Once you have identified the problem to be solved, it's time to focus on providing the solution. How will you address the problem you have identified? This is the "meat and bones" of your business. The business world is highly competitive, so satisfying your customers should always be a top priority. If you can effectively and efficiently solve a major problem in the industry, you will have no shortage of customers.

I discovered that new business owners struggle with understanding and completing business plans. They also did not want to write one, even if they were capable. Our solution was to create very thorough business plans within a reasonable amount of time. We would also help to educate owners on the components of a business plan in the process. Understanding this document is imperative for customers to be able to effectively explain their business plans to investors and lenders during the loan process. After we conduct a few sessions with the client, we will write out the business plan and send the client a digital copy. We also will provide the customer with a hard copy of the business plan. We inform customers that business plans must be reviewed and revised constantly to be truly effective. Therefore, we offer to meet with our clients once a month for additional business coaching. During this monthly meeting, we will compare forecasted numbers against actual performance numbers. We will review the effectiveness of the marketing strategy. We will check to see if short-term goals have been met. As a business coach, my clients understand that my goal is to help them fulfill their business missions.

During the initial coaching session with my clients, I review the business coaching process to determine a solution to their main problem. It is critical to help clients understand exactly what your solution consists of so there is no misunderstanding. Your brand's message should be consistent when you are marketing to customers. Potential clients who have a problem that your business can effectively solve will seek you out. This is the basis of "good business." Once a customer has trusted you with their business, it's time to deliver on your promise. Attracting customers and keeping them are two separate matters. Customers look for effectiveness and efficiency when dealing with businesses. There is a concept called "value delivery;" it is the essence of providing a solution in a way that satisfies the customer. As a business owner, mastering the concept of value delivery will help you to gain repeat customers who eventually refer other customers to your business. To maintain that competitive edge, you should constantly search for methods to improve your solution. Today's business landscape is extremely competitive and innovative, so a good business solution can turn into an average business solution very quickly. This is the reason it is a common occurrence to see companies that were once iconic go bankrupt or completely out of business.

A business plan should be used as a tool for growth and not just for show. Again, it's not made to be created and put on a shelf. "Review" and "revise" should be two words a business owner never forgets. Focus on always providing the best possible solutions and your customers will remain loyal to your brand.

Chapter 8
Get to Know Your Customers

To create and maintain a successful business, you must have extensive knowledge on your target market. You must know which demographics fit within the scope of your target. This is one of the most important components of business planning. If you get this right, you will save yourself a lot of money and time later down the road. Without understanding your target market, it's very difficult to put together an effective marketing strategy. It's very important to understand specific characteristics such as age, location, and median income of your potential clients. If you don't effectively research your target market, how will you know what to charge for your services? How will you know where to advertise? These are essential questions every business owner should ask. The alternative to conducting market research is to just throw ideas against the wall and hope something sticks. You can imagine how that method is very ineffective and expensive. This is a key reason why the majority of new businesses fail in the beginning years. Market research directs your advertising to the right social media platforms.

Contrary to popular belief, Facebook and Instagram may not be the best advertisement platforms for your specific business. Maybe you have not received the best response from your flyers because they are posted at a location your target market rarely frequents. Taking time to conduct market research in the beginning will go a long way to helping your business thrive in a competitive marketplace. My target market consisted of mostly new business owners that were 1-3 years invested in their entrepreneurship. These new business owners struggle with putting together business plans. Their ages ranged from about 20-40 years old. Their businesses operated within or very close to my hometown. The owners were people who had a strong desire to succeed and a passion for helping their local community. They also were very active on social media. Understanding these characteristics about my target market allowed me to assemble a very effective marketing campaign. I began to advertise on social media, catering to new business owners. An important piece of my advertising was offering to help these new entrepreneurs complete full business plans.

Through my market research, I discovered the main thing my target market desired was a complete written business plan. Most of them were applying for business loans, and a completed business plan was a requirement for funding. Giving back to my community is also very important to me. Any real movement should begin from the inside out. So, I begin to network with like-minded individuals who showed sincerity about uplifting our local community. They were individuals who showed their philanthropic intentions through affiliations with community groups and the local Chamber of Commerce. This connection to my community led to opportunities conducting workshops and receiving referrals. I loved it because I was not only growing my business but also helping people in my community grow their own businesses. After concluding a coaching session with my clients, we both would leave the session inspired. It felt like every meeting was meant to happen and each client was sent my way for reasons deeper than business. I'm a very spiritual person and I don't really believe in luck or coincidences. I believe that everything happens for a reason. Another thing that helped me bond with my target market was my ability to relate to most of the life lessons they were experiencing. I started Adam Divine Clothing a couple of years ago, so the strategies that I recommend to my clients are still to be incorporated by our team. The passion they have for the community is a trait I know very well. The setbacks they may be experiencing, I have also experienced. In other words, I'm currently in or trudged through the same trenches as my clients. I just may possess a little more experience and expertise in the business arena.

CHAPTER 9
Not Scared, Just Aware

Identifying and understanding your competition is a key component in the establishment and maintenance of all businesses - especially new businesses. As a new business owner ready to take on the world, you might feel that paying attention to other businesses is not necessary. You might feel so confident in your product or service that you assume focusing on your competitors is a total waste of time. This can be a very costly mistake. Although you should not fear or obsess over your competition, you should be paying attention. There are many benefits in researching the products and services of your competitors. By researching businesses that offer similar services, you may get a clearer understanding on why customers are choosing alternatives. You may discover or hone in on an industry trend that can help you grow your business. Sometimes you must ride the wave of what's working in the market that you serve. Most of the time, successful businesses are not reinventing the wheel. They just find creative ways to take something that is already working and repackage it. Another benefit of researching your competition is discovering something lacking or a component that is not currently being offered. This can be a very important discovery because it may end up becoming your niche. This is common in larger commercial or corporate industries. It is a prime opportunity for new businesses to use their freedom, agility and creativity to capitalize on a specific niche.

For example, when I attained my business coaching certification, I realized that business consultants performed a wide range of services. These services included everything from sales training, mentoring, and marketing to budget coaching. I quickly discovered it would be best for me to find a niche, master it and lead that particular industry in my area. As I begin to research the competitors in my local area, I realized they provided a wide range of services, but these services didn't really cater to new businesses. Their services mainly accommodated larger corporations and tackled strategy, employee training and life coaching. What I didn't see were consultants specializing in helping business owners create and understand the nuts and bolts of a business plan. From my research, I discovered that business planning was a task that new business owners in my area struggled to execute. Some businesses needed to create business plans to receive funding. Others sought business plans for direction because they felt "stuck" after registering their new business. So, I thought to myself, *why not provide a service that helps new business owners comprehend all the components of a business plan?* This would provide each of them a roadmap to navigate their business journey and give them a tool to grow and expand their business. I also guaranteed them complete written business plans at the end of the process. If they needed outside funding, they would each possess a solid business plan to present to future investors and bankers. I knew immediately that I had found my niche. I also gained a better understanding of who fit in my target market. After this discovery, I set out to learn all aspects of business planning. My expertise began to grow along with my confidence. I built my home on a specific spot within the business coaching island. Since I understood who I was as a business coach, my marketing spoke specifically to my target market. To my surprise, there was a great deal of business owners seeking the specific service I offered. More clients than I could manage began to seek my niche services; I even began seriously contemplating my exit plan from my corporate job. Most of this was made possible because I conducted market research and studied my competitors.

By identifying a service my competitors were not offering, I stumbled upon my niche. Again, there can be many benefits which materialize from researching your competition.

CHAPTER 10
Quality Over Everything

In the article "In the End Your Business Boils Down to This," Tom Ewer says, "most business experts will tell you that businesses typically compete on one or two levels - price and quality or both." When I made the decision to start my clothing line, I had to determine how I would separate myself from the competition. My business reputation was vital, and I wanted to take pride in providing excellent service to my customers. I wanted my clothing line to be known for being original, creative and providing quality products. From the very start, one thing I realized is that your reputation as a business owner will either become an asset or a liability. When I started Adam Divine Clothing, I researched many different business components such as clothing manufacturers, distribution channels, etc. One of the key decisions I had to make was choosing a wholesale manufacturer. It really came down to deciding whether our business would focus more on price or quality. Even prior to my business being registered and my trademark becoming official, I decided that providing quality products would be a staple of my business.

I would raise my prices to cover purchasing and operating costs, rather than buying cheaper material, which creates a watered-down product. One thing I realized is customers don't mind paying higher prices for quality products; they will invest in products or services they feel are worth their money. This was also an easy decision because part of Adam Divine Clothing's mission statement stands by this standard; it describes our company as striving for excellence and providing quality products. Every business owner should make providing quality products and services a top priority. After all, customers are giving their hard-earned money in exchange for something valuable. Some of my most rewarding experiences being a business owner occur when I get the opportunity to speak with satisfied customers. To hear them enthusiastically express their overall satisfaction with our products and services reinforces our mission statement. Now what if I would have chosen a cheaper product or used less durable material for my clothing line? This could have been a nightmare for our reputation. We could have instantly lost the trust of these customers who may have never purchased from us again.

Furthermore, it is common knowledge in most industries that word of mouth is a strong source of advertisement. Many customers have organically advertised for me by simply speaking highly of our products and services. There have been many instances when potential customers have spotted me in public and expressed genuine excitement about others wearing our products. In each of these instances, they provided great reviews. This almost always led to additional sales without any additional advertisement. I will always provide my customers with a fair price, but I would rather be known most for providing quality products. Of course, this strategy may lead to our products retailing at higher price points in comparison to some of our competition. However, excellence and quality are attributes we take pride in providing. As a business owner, I encourage you to never sacrifice quality to make additional profits. You may see monetary benefits for a moment, but eventually you will damage your reputation, which will begin to negatively affect all areas of your business. Remember, "owning your passion" consists of having the courage and privilege to share your story with the world, so take pride in making sure every business experience is positive and beneficial to everyone involved.

CHAPTER 11
Welcome to The Club

Another benefit of becoming an entrepreneur is having the privilege to join a network of business owners. Business owners are some of the most ambitious and courageous people you will encounter. In the article "20 Reasons to Start Your Own Business," Mike Templeman states, "Your circle of friends and acquaintances always grows when you become an entrepreneur, as many founders need others to lean on to survive and talk about the challenges only known to them." When you become an entrepreneur, you will automatically enter a network of individuals you may have never otherwise met in life. A successful business is a mechanism that depends on multiple components involving a variety of individuals. Whether it is suppliers, contractors, employees, or customers, being a business owner allows you the ability to cultivate wonderful new relationships. Prior to discovering my true niche, I was involved in a few different business ventures. I recall needing some flyers and business cards printed, so I was referred to a local printing shop. I remember noticing that this shop displayed various clothing items of completed screen print work on the walls. Ten years later, the day I decided to start my clothing line, I needed someone to create a digital image of my company logo. I remembered the previous work this shop completed, so I gave them a call to see if they could handle the job. Amazingly, they were able to bring the logo to life, and not long after, it became a registered trademark. Whether it involves preparation for a fashion show, or a custom-designed product, I can depend on them to provide quality screen printing work. Over the years, I have built and maintained a great business relationship with the owner and employees. Developing a good relationship with Arrow Printing has led to many benefits, such as flexibility in pricing and reasonable payment arrangements when necessary. Being a successful business owner requires time, patience, and grit, so strong strategic partnerships are essential for success. These connections can be one of the main factors that determine success or failure. Operating a business is an extremely complex process and having experienced partnerships on your side to help simplify things is a blessing. One of the beauties of establishing business relationships is being able to meet people from all different walks of life, with different cultures and backgrounds. This will help you to develop a clearer perspective from a business standpoint. There are contractors already affiliated with similar businesses within your industry, so they can provide you with helpful industry advice. In my case, this has been advantageous in relation to design input and wholesale contracting. I received invaluable guidance and consulting from my contractors on properly choosing the appropriate wholesale manufacturer. Even though they are contractors and not official employees, I consider Arrow Printing to be part of the Adam Divine

Team. They produce quality work, and they were affiliated with my brand from the beginning, witnessing and contributing to its growth. Even if growth forced me to produce my clothing products on a scale beyond their realm of capabilities, I would still find a way to conduct business with them in some form or fashion. That is the level of appreciation I have for their expertise, quality of work and flexibility. I was recently speaking with a close friend about the power of networking, and I mentioned how much I enjoy organic networking. I consider organic networking to be interactions between businesses without any hidden agendas. Both parties can assist each other by providing something beneficial to one another. This natural method leads to mutual respect and great appreciation. Respect is developed because most entrepreneurs understand both the hardships and successes that every business owner encounters. These may be individuals with whom you can share a cup of coffee or trade ideas over lunch.

Again, one of the perks of owning your passion is meeting people who may become business partners, mentors, and in rare instances, real genuine friends. Networking organically with the right individuals is a major benefit for entrepreneurs. It's amazing how your true passion will connect you with like-minded associates, which may lead to healthy long-term business relationships.

I decided that after I finished writing my book, I would treat myself to a trip to Las Vegas for a few days. I had never visited Vegas, and it also gave me a chance to reconnect with an uncle I hadn't seen in years. As the passengers boarded the plane, I was seated in a middle seat between two other passengers. My first thought was about the duration of the four-hour flight, so I would use the opportunity to get some rest - at least that's what I *thought* would happen. I introduced myself to the gentleman to the left of me. He said he was traveling back to Vegas after being home in Michigan for the past year. He said he previously owned a cell phone business in Las Vegas for over 12 years. I told him that I was a business coach/owner and I was on the cusp of releasing my first book. I asked him if he wouldn't mind sharing a few business tips with me since he had a ton of practical experience. I respected his ability to maintain a business for 12 years. With the high rate of failure for new businesses, I knew he had to be doing something right during his time of business ownership. As we conversed, I could sense he was a very knowledgeable, ambitious and humble guy. After he briefly shared his story, he asked for my opinion on starting and operating a successful business. This was a segue for me to go into detail about what I do, and how I help my clients. I touched on the importance of identifying your individual passion and using a business plan as a tool and not a trophy. I spoke in detail about the importance of strategic business planning. Before you know it, we were discussing business and sharing stories for at least three hours. He laughed and expressed how he wished we encountered each other back when he was operating his previous business. He felt he could have been a lot more successful. This gentleman is now currently starting a new business more closely aligned with his passion. I have no doubt that he will be successful. It was encouraging to receive a compliment from an experienced business owner. Unknowingly, the gentleman to my right was listening to our entire conversation. He joined in on the conversation, and I learned that he was a graphic designer from a family of entrepreneurs. He said his father owned a successful insurance company and his brother was an aspiring business owner who had a lot of great ideas.

He took my business card and said he would like for me to work with his brother. The three of us discussed life and business for the duration of the entire flight. Before you know it, we heard a voice announcing we would be landing in Vegas shortly. Amazingly, from the time it took to travel from Detroit to Las Vegas, I had acquired two new business clients and formed two new connections that had the potential to benefit all parties involved. I don't know about having the gift of gab, but I do have a passion for building prosperous businesses and helping others do the same. When you truly "own your passion," God has a way of connecting people who can benefit each other in multiple ways. Consider it a blessing when God puts the right people in your path at the right time. Networking and sharing your passion with others are just two of the many benefits of becoming a business owner.

CHAPTER 12
Free at Last

Without a doubt, one of the greatest benefits of entrepreneurship is having the ability to creatively pursue your vision. Elizabeth Venafro, co-founder and managing partner of True Exec stated "Entrepreneurship represents the opportunity to make something from nothing. There are no rules and no limitations. You set your own boundaries." The joy that comes from truly owning your passion is indescribable. Being a business owner allows you to truly create something from nothing. To see your idea and vision evolve from a mere thought to an actual business is nothing short of amazing. God has truly blessed me to be able to develop a clothing line, start a business coaching practice, and become an author. From the beginning, my vision was to create a brand that represented creativity and originality. I wanted the Adam Divine brand to represent excellence and inspire others to use their God-given abilities in an innovative and productive fashion. Receiving positive feedback from satisfied customers is rewarding and a great source of reinforcement. Not very many people will understand the courage and hard work it takes to become a successful business owner. Late last year, I was working out at a local gym. I was riding on one of the stationary bikes, when I glanced over to the other side of the gym and spotted an older gentleman of a different ethnicity wearing a T-shirt from my clothing line. At first, I thought it was just a competitor's shirt donning a similar logo, but when you put blood, sweat and tears into a project, you can recognize your work from miles away. It was gratifying to see someone much older than myself, and of a different ethnicity representing my brand. I walked over to the gentleman and said, "That's a nice shirt you have on there." He smiled and said, "Yeah, I believe my son bought it for me and I definitely like it." I then introduced myself and thanked him and his family for their support. It was really a wonderful moment and it inspired me even more to continue sharing my story with the world. And I purposely used the phrase "sharing my story with the world," because I believe being an entrepreneur consists of effectively sharing your story with the world. Sharing your story with the world may come in the form of providing a quality product or delivering a great service. When it comes to being a successful business owner, you creatively decide to share with others an idea that was once merely an intimate thought. Doing this should bring you joy, being able to creatively share your vision at the appropriate time. This is something that I truly thank God for because I have seen the vision come to life in a short period of time. As a current business owner or someone who is just preparing to start your entrepreneurial journey, the ability to bring your vision to light is a privilege and one amazing experience.

CHAPTER 13
Don't Forget About You

In this section, I will discuss the significance of investing in you. This can initially be done in an inexpensive way. Applying this principle has helped me tremendously. As business owners, we rightfully invest in our business which does pay major dividends. For example, buying a new laptop or tablet for my coaching profession would be an example of investing in my business; because upgrading supplies and equipment can improve and enhance the way I generate and conduct business. However, when I suggest that you invest in yourself, I'm referring to a more intimate investment. This may include purchasing and reading books on business, tuning in to podcasts, finding a mentor, hiring a business coach or taking a much-needed vacation.

Teaching business principles to aspiring business owners has always been a part of my vision. Although I hold a degree in business management, I wanted to develop a more specific skill set related to my future occupation. I didn't really want or have the time to enroll in a traditional business school to further my education in this area. Unfortunately, traditional schooling doesn't always prepare a person to master a specific skill set. It has been through actual experience that I have learned the value and benefit of specialization. Becoming certified in business coaching is an investment I made in myself to fulfill my desire to teach and guide others. My first order of business was to research the top employment certification institutions in the business field.

It was in the business-coaching course that I learned valuable coaching fundamentals. This allowed me to develop a particular skill set that would serve my future clients well. I wanted to be equipped to provide business owners with practical knowledge they could use to instantly grow their business. Increasing my skill set and obtaining a reputable certification that externally showed my willingness to invest in myself, were essential steps in the process to build a business that services the needs of others. I wanted my clients to know that they are in good hands. I always had a passion for teaching business, so starting a coaching business felt inevitable. My plan was to become a successful business owner first and then naturally move into business coaching. I always held the belief that it's much more respectable to teach something that you have successfully experienced. After I created Adam Divine Clothing and experienced some success, I felt it was the right time to enter the business-coaching arena. Finding various ways to increase your skill set is an excellent way to invest in you. Once I received my business coaching certification, I immediately created an LLC and began to market my new services. I decided to focus on a specific niche as a coach and assist small business owners with completing business plans. As an entrepreneur, I knew that creating a business plan was one of the most crucial things to establish for a business owner. My intuition served me well. Shortly after marketing my services, I gained new clientele and received requests to conduct business-planning workshops. This all happened because I made the conscious decision to invest in myself. Reading books is another inexpensive way to invest in you. This can include books on leadership or books directly related to your specific business. Books and other literature, such as articles or blogs allow us to attain wisdom from scholars and experts we would not have the opportunity to meet under normal circumstances. One of my favorite business books is *The Personal MBA* by Josh Kaufman. This piece of work has been instrumental in my development as a businessman. One cardinal lesson I learned from this book was the importance of understanding the fundamental components of a business. Kaufman states, "Roughly defined, a business is a repeatable process that: 1. Creates and delivers something of value. 2. That other people want or need. 3. At a price they're willing to pay. 4. In a way that satisfies the customer's needs and expectations. 5. So that the business brings in enough profit to make it worthwhile for the owners to continue operation. Understanding this simplified concept of what a business truly is helped me understand specific business components such as value creation, marketing, sales, value delivery, and finance. By becoming more knowledgeable about these business components, I was able to more effectively focus on and improve my business.

The title of the book is *The Personal MBA* because the author believes that you can master the art of business without mortgaging your life in the process. This is one of my most frequently used resources when I want to study specific business concepts. Whether it's related to marketing, sales or finance, I can immediately apply what I've learned. At the time of this writing, you can purchase *The Personal MBA* for less than $20 in the U.S. How is that for investing in you? That was a small price to invest in a product that has paid huge dividends. We live in the information age where you can acquire valuable information for a relatively low cost or even for free. As business owners, we buy so many products and services to help ensure success in a very competitive marketplace; but we must never forget that the most important investment is to invest in ourselves.

CHAPTER 14
It's Game Time

Whether it's starting a new business or beginning that new workout plan, truth is there will never be a perfect time. Waiting on the perfect time can lead to procrastination or completely missing out on your opportunity altogether. An effective habit to develop is visualizing a goal in full completion, and then focusing only on the next step needed to bring you closer to the end goal. After becoming a business coach, I wanted to focus on something that would provide additional value to my clients. After conducting research, I became determined to write a book encouraging business owners to follow their dreams. My goal was to inspire them to own their passion. My goal was for the book to be both inspirational and applicable. The central idea was to provide practical information on how to create a sound business plan. The decision had been made mentally, but I didn't know where to start. Writing a book seemed like a huge project that would take years to complete. I was unsure if I had what it took to write a book. A good friend encouraged me to listen to some motivational and instructional videos by Tony Gaskins. Tony Gaskins is a very successful life coach, speaker, author and businessman. He was conducting a course called "Birth Your Book," which helped aspiring authors to write and publish their first book. The course helped the reader break down writing a book into very simple and doable steps. The steps were all in order and easy to follow. This includes learning the value of setting a specific time each day to write. It's amazing what you can accomplish when you follow an actual plan.

I set a time to write for at least an hour each day. Knowing I was on my way to becoming an author was an amazing feeling. What was even more significant was realizing I was working on creating a product that could inspire someone to move closer to their dreams. Purchasing "Birth Your Book" was the first step I needed to take to begin the process of becoming an author. Two things stood out to me in the "Birth Your Book" course. Tony mentioned the importance of making a point and telling a story related to that point. Before I knew it, I was about ten pages deep in writing the book you are reading now. This happened because I focused on just completing the very "next step" to becoming an author. When you set a large goal, it becomes almost impossible to accomplish in one setting. The concept of consistently focusing on the next step will help you move closer and closer to reaching your goal. Every step you complete will help you gain the momentum that will eventually carry you to the finish line. Almost everybody has at least one book in them because we all have a unique story. However, too many dreams fall to the wayside and are wasted, because we don't learn how to break down large projects into manageable actions. Focus on the very next step and take action. Before you know it, that huge project will be completed through smaller stages. Some people will wonder how you finished such an enormous project. You can let them know you did it by religiously completing one step at a time.

CHAPTER 15
Seize the Moment

Deuteronomy 8:18 – "But you shall remember the LORD your God: for it is he that gives you the power to get wealth, that he may establish his covenant which he swore to your fathers, as it is this day." Attaining wealth is not for you to become arrogant and gluttonous. It's not for you to forget the God who blessed you with the ability to produce wealth in the first place. No, it's not for you to begin consuming drugs and alcohol or engage in inappropriate relations, which eventually will lead to destruction. God has blessed some of us with divine abilities that will allow us to become very successful entrepreneurs. This ability will create something that will improve the lives of many. It will make it possible for entrepreneurs to support their families and be an inspiration to others. For those of us who fall into this category, we should humbly count it as a blessing and do everything possible to productively use this ability. I grew up in an environment that was full of challenges.

Some of these challenges were of the spiritual, social and financial nature. My childhood neighborhoods were filled with drugs, violence and poverty. I've seen good people do terrible things for money. I've seen the lack of finances cause people to take terrible chances that led to long prison terms and death. The lack of true financial literacy has destroyed a lot of families. I know some people who think illegal activities are the only way to generate a substantial amount of income. My question for you is what if God has given you a special ability to become a successful businessperson? What if this ability is designed for you to take care of your family and break generational curses that may have negatively affected your family and community? What if you have been blessed with this ability to inspire future entrepreneurs to do the same? If you fit this category, the time to act is now. How do you know if you fit this category? You should feel it deep in your soul. I felt it that day at Starbucks when I begin praying to God about something missing in my life. Shortly after, Adam Divine LLC was created. Massive action must follow once you realize you were blessed with the desire and the ability to become an entrepreneur. We each have a specific season to accomplish certain goals and perform certain deeds within this lifetime.

There is a season to wait and then there is a season to act. When it's your season to act, please don't hesitate and miss out on your blessings. When it became my season, I reached a point of clarity and realization. In all aspects of my life, things seem to be falling naturally in place. I started Adam Divine Clothing a couple of years ago. I started Adam Divine Business Coaching almost two years later. This wasn't a concrete plan, but the timing felt right to embark on my career as a business coach. My intuition turned out to be very accurate. There was a business coaching need for entrepreneurs in my local community. My passion seamlessly matched up with this need. Again, it's not a case of coincidences; God's hand was guiding the entire process. I began helping business owners complete their business plans and conducting workshops which led to another intuitive decision. It became time to write a book aiming to share my story with aspiring entrepreneurs. Throughout my recent business journey, I have been blessed with a sense of timing and courage, which has opened many doors that were previously closed. This is my time to courageously act and pursue the things I previously envisioned. Please own or develop this same sense of urgency. Tomorrow is not promised to any of us. Even amid doubt or fear we must still move forward. Courage may be defined as moving forward in the face of fear.

This season of action will bless my family and me for years to come. It will also bless others who God put in my territory to teach and mentor. I realize that if I don't act now, these opportunities may never come around again. Each of us is blessed in more ways than we can imagine. However, there are certain blessings that are seasonal. Never let fear or any other distraction cause you to miss your season. Don't miss out on what God has for you now.

About five years ago, I was in the worst spiritual, emotional, and financial state of my life. Fast forward and God has blessed me to become a minister, clothing designer, business coach and now an author. After you weather the storm, your season for productivity and prosperity will eventually come. Will you seize the moment, or will you make excuses based on fear? I encourage you as a business owner to constantly pray and move when God says move. Based on those two principles, my life has totally changed for the better. Everybody has what I consider their "8 mile" moment. "8 Mile" was a popular song and movie starring rapper Eminem, based on the beginning of his rap career. It displayed the success and failures of his musical journey in beautiful fashion. One of the main points of the movie was the importance of being ready to seize the moment when that once-in-a-lifetime opportunity presents itself. For Eminem, that moment occurred when he had to compete with other rappers in front of very large and critical audiences. This is the moment when you get the chance to prove you belong in your desired arena. It's the moment that will change your life completely if you seize it. How do you seize the moment? Just ask yourself, *what is the next step I need to take to move me closer to my dream?* Courageously take that next step and repeat the process. How much you will accomplish in a year or two will completely amaze you. When opportunity knocks at your doorstep, embrace it with a warrior attitude. Thank God for the opportunity and show your gratitude by becoming a business owner who supplies the world with an excellent product or service.

CHAPTER 16
Build an Empire

After you launch your company it's very easy to become satisfied and content. Some business owners get content with simply being in business. It's true that most businesses fail within the first couple of years. However, simply surviving should not be the number one goal of a business owner. Thriving should be the aim. We were each created with something special inside of us and we should not limit ourselves to anything other than greatness. Daniel Ally wrote an article titled "7 steps I followed to build my business empire." A wise man once said, "Why build a candy store when you can build a candy empire?" We have all heard the saying, "If you're going to dream, you should dream big." Dreaming big doesn't necessarily mean to be greedy or bite off more than you can chew. But if you can provide a great product or service to a hundred, why not provide it to thousands? Much of it comes down to learning how to develop the proper systems that make mass production possible. It also boils down to having the right mindset and believing in your individual purpose. Don't settle for a small company when you may have been chosen to create an empire. The concept of thinking big is more about mindset than revenue. In other words, why serve a few if you have been chosen to serve a multitude?

The Adam Divine Clothing motto is **Be Original - Be Creative - Be You!** A clothing line was the initial channel I used to spread this message. The objective was to develop quality clothing that expressed creativity and originality. However, my vision was never limited to a clothing line. The goal was to eventually teach others how to become successful entrepreneurs. This would allow me to help them to follow their dreams and own their passion. I wanted to inspire entrepreneurs to embrace their originality and creativity in their own unique way. This inspired the birth of my coaching business, Adam Divine Business Coaching. The message is identical for all my businesses, but the channels are different. Once I realized the benefits of writing, it was time to deliver the same message through a book. You are now reading a book published by Adam Divine Publishing.

Throughout the process of this business journey, I have developed the urge to create documentaries and films in the future. My vision is to deliver the same original message through this channel. This will allow us to reach a wider more visual audience. Adam Divine Films has been created to address this need. A friend of mine who possesses a passion for producing visual media has access to all the equipment necessary to produce short commercials and documentaries. I instantly noticed the enthusiasm he had for his craft. With the clothing line and business coaching business growing rapidly, I wanted to really capture the moment and share this inspirational story with the world. A short story or documentary would be a creative, visual way to share my journey. Since my friend was passionate about sharpening his skill, he was the best choice to direct the first film project for my new company. He would get the experience and credit for doing the work, and I would share my story under the new film company. This was a win/win situation that benefitted all parties and created exposure on another platform. Remember, I was never interested in just creating a company. One of the goals has always been to build an empire. Not an empire focused on bringing in the most revenue, but one that focuses on reaching a wide array of people. If you focus on consistently providing great value, bringing in money will never be an issue. My desire is to consistently provide quality products through multiple platforms. These products will always be true to the Adam Divine brand. This will lead to a network of other aspiring clothing designers, authors, and filmmakers who may need an avenue to publish their work.

For example, if I was speaking with someone who wanted to write their first book, not only could I offer this person helpful tips, but there could be the opportunity to publish the book under Adam Divine Publishing. The same opportunity would be available for future fashion designers and filmmakers. Having access to multiple platforms will empower entrepreneurs in my community or anyone God puts in my path in need of help. Sometimes we limit ourselves due to fear and insecurities. You may be destined for great things, greater than you may have ever envisioned. As you continue your business journey, keep your eyes open for natural opportunities meant for your growth and expansion. You never know, you may be destined to create a business empire meant to serve a mass customer base in need of your product.

Chapter 17
Approach it Like A Marathon

In a 1995 interview, Steve Jobs said, "I'm convinced that about half of what separates the successful entrepreneurs from the non-successful ones is pure perseverance; no matter how great your product or service is, there is no substitution for hard work." Even if you're super talented, there still is no substitute for a great work ethic. From my research, a great work ethic seems to be a common trait amongst successful entrepreneurs. Many people easily think of great ideas, but most refuse to put in the work required to turn those ideas into success. Let's face it - becoming a successful business owner is not easy. If it was, there would not be such a high failure rate amongst startup companies. Writing a book is not easy. Building a profitable business from the ground up is not easy. Becoming a top athlete is not easy. If any one of those things was easy, everyone would be successful. This is a key reason why most people never reach their goals. It has less to do with talent or ability than most outsiders would believe. Usually it boils down to the lack of grit and the refusal to put in the work necessary to accomplish goals. This became evident to me when I played college basketball.

When I concluded my high school basketball career, I was awarded a few honors. I was considered one of the best point guards in the state of Michigan. My confidence was high, and I was ready to take on the world of Division 1 college basketball. I earned a full athletic scholarship to further my athletic career at Kent State University. This was a huge accomplishment for both my family and me. Since I was not the biggest basketball player, out-working my opponent and being tougher was vital to my success. Skill also played a role, but in many situations, talent can be a little overrated. Once I got to the college campus, I immediately began to size up the competition. Everyone who played my position was considered an enemy in some respect. My short-term goal was to earn a starting position and then become the top point guard in our basketball conference. So, anybody or anything that was blocking that path, in my opinion, was an obstacle. As we begin to play pre-season recreational ball, I noticed that most of these guys were talented, but it was nothing to call home about. They were physically more mature, and I could see the results of good training and conditioning. One day, all the players were provided with a media guide and it listed each players' athletic backgrounds and previous accomplishments.

I carefully read everyone's accomplishments, and something became very apparent to me. All of the players at this level were very accomplished and decorated. They were considered some of the best players in their county and state. Some were recognized for being amongst the best players in the country. If everyone on this basketball team had similar abilities, what was the main thing that separated the best from the rest? I would soon receive my answer. We started conditioning, which included weightlifting and workouts on the track. I began to get a sense of who competed harder than others. On the track, there were those who habitually trailed in the back of the pack because of poor off-season training. In the weight room, some guys maintained a higher level of intensity than others. They maintained this intensity at all times, even when the coaches weren't watching. As we began to practice on the basketball court, a few of the guys consistently played harder than the rest. They ran the floor harder, they cut to the basket harder, they played harder defense, and always brought a mental toughness that stood out. It became apparent to me that the best players on the team were the ones who had the best work ethic. We all were talented, but in a pool of talented players, a strong work ethic was the distinguishing factor. There are only a few Michael Jordan's & Lebron James's in the world. Whether its basketball or business, developing a strong work ethic is one of the most effective and significant things you can ever do. Talent will only take you so far, and in some cases, it may hurt you in the long run. Talent can often cause some people to become arrogant and develop a sense of entitlement. How many stories have we seen or heard about the star athlete who never fulfilled his potential? How many times have we seen people with average ability get a promotion over their more talented peers? How is this possible? Research strongly suggests it comes down to possessing and maintaining a strong, consistent work ethic.

This is a crucial fact in the business arena right now. More than likely, you are not going to create any groundbreaking products or services. What you can do, however, is consistently provide superior customer service in comparison to your competitors. You can increase your skill level by reading more books and attending more industry-related seminars. Or, you can spend more time researching your market to find more effective ways to serve your customers. You can constantly review your business plan to assess what's working and what's not. You might have to alter your marketing strategy or eliminate unnecessary expenses. This is called "work," and if you want success, you must commit to outworking the competition. The positive side is most business owners are already engaged in something they are passionate about.

True passion is a huge advantage, but it still doesn't substitute for hard work. Hard work is not the only ingredient to success, but it is difficult to sustain success without it. Make a commitment to work hard and always do your best. The key is to not only work harder than your competitors, but to also develop the ability to work longer than your competitors. Failure and success often come down to whether you perceive your journey to be a sprint or a marathon.

CHAPTER 18
Your Future Is in Your Circle

How refreshing is it to be surrounded by people who support and encourage you on a consistent basis? It's vital to you as an entrepreneur and even more critical to you as a person. Life is already tough, and becoming a successful businessperson is a whole different challenge in itself. Therefore, it's imperative to surround yourself with people who will uplift you on a consistent basis. This is one of the reasons business owners tend to associate with other business owners. Although they may specialize in different industries, they understand the work required to operate a successful business. Mutual respect is developed, and encouragement is naturally offered between business owners. Encouragement can come in many forms. It can be constructive criticism about your product from a family member or friend. You accept it because you realize that they love you and truly want to see you prosper. All successful business owners realize that feedback from those on the outside is a tremendous benefit. Some of the most valuable market research is customer feedback. Be proactive and ask your customers for their honest opinions about your business. You will be surprised by how much this will help your business in the long run. Maintaining a circle of loyal customers and affiliates is vital because their support will be a key component to your success.

Also, people who sincerely support you will refer others to you when they believe in your business. When I launched Adam Divine Clothing, most of my initial business came from referrals. I was still working in the corporate world and a few of my co-workers purchased some of my designer t-shirts. They wore the shirts with pride, unknowingly becoming walking billboards promoting my company. I would have been satisfied with that gesture alone, but fortunately, it didn't stop there. They enthusiastically spread the word about my new business venture. They always sang my praises and mentioned my company in a positive light.

The people in my circle were very passionate about the product. Some people genuinely want to see you succeed. These people are very rare and must be appreciated and acknowledged for their support. These are the type of individuals with whom you should intentionally surround yourself. Your gift to them should be to encourage them and offer the same type of support they offer you. This literally will become a virtuous cycle of positivity that can create a very powerful movement. I like to refer to this type of environment as the "winner's circle." Realistically, most people are probably not going to wish you well in your business endeavors. That's just the reality of life. You never know what others are personally experiencing that may be manifesting a spirit of envy or jealousy. What's important is for you to separate yourself and your business from it, and do not waste time or energy on negativity that has the potential to infect your climb to success. Instead your time should be spent being grateful and supporting those who support you. Be sure to let them know how much you appreciate their support and creatively look for ways to reward them. This could be anything from treating them to a night out to dine together, or simply encouraging them to use their gifts and abilities to create a better life. The truth is that everyone will need the help of somebody at some point in time, especially in the business world. Entrepreneurship is truly an interdependent vocation. This includes everyone from family, friends, vendors, contractors and customers. As a current or aspiring business owner, you will face an unknown number of adversities on your journey to success. One of the most powerful weapons you can possess is the support of those who genuinely want to see you succeed. This may only consist of a handful of people, but your "winner's circle" will be extremely valuable to your peace and success. Anybody or anything that consistently takes away from your peace and prosperity should be distanced immediately. As a business owner, you also must make sure you become a positive light in the lives of others. Provide encouragement and constructive criticism in a spirit of love. Surround yourself with positive, supportive individuals, and you will reap great benefits in both your personal life and business life. There is great joy in being a part of a "winner's circle."

CHAPTER 19
Don't Be Afraid of Success

Most of the time, we discuss how destructive it is to live with a fear of failure; however, some experts believe that the fear of success may be more devastating than its counterpart. Everybody desires success, right? So, who in their right mind would be afraid to succeed? There are many of us who fall in this category, whether we admit or not.

Before my senior year of college basketball at Alabama State University, we were very optimistic heading into the new season. We had a very talented roster and a nice mixture of veterans and underclassmen. Our freshmen class was extremely talented, and many figured we had a good chance of making it to the NCAA tournament. We were facing a tough non-conference schedule that included the likes of traditional powers such as Alabama, Arkansas, Ole Miss and DePaul. This particular year, DePaul had one of the best freshman classes in the country. This freshman class included two future NBA players, Quentin Richardson & Bobby Simmons. We were super excited to play this tough non-conference schedule. We felt winning the games gave us a chance to put our school on the college basketball map. Individually, a few of us had aspired to play professional basketball. We embraced the opportunity to compete against more highly rated players. However, circumstances didn't quite pan out like we wanted in these marquee games. We were competitive in most of these games and provided a couple teams with a major scare. The problem? We displayed a pattern of putting ourselves in position to win, but never did quite enough to pull out the win. We had the opportunity to pull off the impossible, but we consistently let it slip away in the end. After one of these games, our head coach was giving his traditional end-of-the-game speech. After a loss, the speech is always brutal for players to hear. I don't remember the speech verbatim, but I do remember one thing my coach said which has stuck with me for over 20 years. I remember it like it was yesterday. He looked at us with a unique mixture of calm, disappointment and intensity. He said, "I know what the problem is now; this team is scared of success." He didn't talk about the typical things like playing stronger offense, defense or putting in more effort. In his mind, he had unfortunately figured out the root problem with our team.

We were talented, but we were afraid of success. As I was sitting there deflated from the loss, I remember experiencing mixed emotions and confusion about what I just heard. I thought to myself, *who in their right mind would fear success?* We all have a desire to be successful, right? Whether its athletics, academics, parenting, entrepreneurship, it is a common belief that everyone wants to be successful. Although I was a little confused by his statement, a nagging feeling in my soul told me

84

there was some truth to what he said. Now that I've overcome a few life obstacles and experienced some level of business success, the revelation of my former coach's statement has become clear. The truth is, for many different reasons, many people are consciously or unconsciously afraid of success.

Why would someone be afraid of success? Unfortunately, there are negative things that tend to follow success - envy and jealousy. For whatever reason, successful individuals often receive unjust criticism from negative people. This is not discussing criticism that is justified; constructive criticism is effective for all of us. When it is productive, and the purpose is motivation, it is something that can elevate us to greater heights. This is about jealousy and envy that sprout up out of a purely evil spirit. You need to understand that this type of negativity is never about you. Yeah, you read that correctly – it's not about you. When this type of energy is sent your way for no reason, it's typically because that sender is grappling with something internally. One of the lessons in the book, *The Four Agreements,* by Don Miguel Ruiz states, "Don't take anything personally." It elaborates that nothing another person does is because of you, it's always because of that person.

Also, sometimes we stop short of success because of past shortcomings. It's amazing how the ugly past will choke the life out of many people's future. You may be right at the brink of success and the past will rear its ugly head. Years of work may get thrown down the drain because you are afraid to take that last important step. Success may be calling your name, but you allow the loud voice of negativity to drown out your calling. Previous disappointments could include past abuse, previous failures or anything that caused serious pain. What's sad is that in many instances, there are people who become content with a life of failure. Unfortunately, some people become more comfortable with failure than success. Success is uncharted territory for most individuals. We all know how situations that take us out of our comfort zones can sometimes be fearful.

They key is to continue doing what you were destined to even amid fear. That is a major sign of bravery. Eventually, you will become more at ease in this unchartered territory of success.

Another reason some people are afraid of success is they feel unworthy of the accolades. They fear the world may find out that they are not as skillful or talented as some are projecting them to be. Remember, no one is perfect, but you must continue to work at your crafts. Always do your absolute best and find ways to increase your skill level whenever possible. Work with integrity and do what you say you are going to do. Operating with integrity will cause your customers to respect and appreciate you. That respect will create loyal consumerism and a fine reputation. Always search for ways to provide extra value to your customers. If you develop and maintain a growth mindset, you will more than satisfy your customers. With this approach, you will begin to naturally reach above and beyond your clients' expectations. Remember Jesus Christ lived a perfect life and He still was heavily criticized. So, never let any just or unjust criticism stop you from taking hold of what God has for you. Remember, walking in your purpose is part of being free. Whether spiritually, mentally, or physically, there is nothing acceptable about voluntarily remaining in chains. In other words, when success calls your name, gratefully and courageously answer the call.

Lastly, one of the ways to overcome fear of success is to keep your eyes focused on the big picture. Make sure you consistently visualize what your success looks like. Does it consist of you being able to spend more time with your family? Does it allow you to travel more and have amazing experiences outside of your everyday environment? Does it provide you with financial freedom? Does it allow you to spend more time giving back to your community? Your success will often inspire those who are watching from afar. Many haters will come out of the weeds; however, God tends to provide the right amount of supporters to offset their negativity. That support is always available at the perfect time. Always remember why you wanted to become a business owner in the first place. You must "own your passion." Do not fear success in any shape or fashion. Most likely, you have been waiting for this moment all your life. Embrace the joy and pain of the journey and remember that nothing can compare with the joy and peace of living out your purpose. You were absolutely born to be successful.

CHAPTER 20
The Many Benefits of Having A Mentor

As a business owner, having a mentor brings about many benefits. One of the benefits is receiving invaluable and timely advice. There will be times during your business venture when your trusted advisor, with experience in your chosen industry, will have the perfect answers to your questions. These questions can range from topics such as launching a new product to changing your marketing strategy. At the start of my clothing line, I was very eager and ambitious. I was proud of the progress I made in such a short period of time. I spent a great deal of time researching the clothing industry before I launched my clothing line. I studied everything from clothing materials, distribution, marketing etc. However, as the business began to progress, I realized that I would benefit greatly from eliciting the expertise of a good mentor with experience in the fashion industry. The ironic thing was I had just obtained a financial lawyer who was assisting me on a personal level. I was very impressed with his expertise and professionalism. I advised him that I had recently started a new business and things were really progressing. During this time, I was in the process of trademarking my business logo. Everything was moving along smoothly until the very end of the trademark process. I received government notification that a large company had opposed my trademark registration at the tail end of the process. This simply meant that the opposing company believed our logos were similar enough to cause customer confusion when differentiating between the two. The funny thing was the logos were not identical at all, but their company's logo also contained the word "Adam." The opposing company requested a settlement I was not comfortable with accepting. Agreeing to this settlement would have significantly limited the future growth of my business. I sought the advice of the aforementioned lawyer who had experience in these situations and he advised me of my options. Feeling much more confident about the situation, I took his advice and we all were able to reach a resolution in the end. The way my lawyer was able to assist and advise me made a tremendous impression. I approached him about the possibility of becoming my business mentor and he accepted and agreed to a working relationship where he could provide me with any additional advice to help me in the future. A good mentor will openly provide you with quality advice in times of need.

A good mentor will help to open networking opportunities for you. They will help you create and expand your current network. When you begin to meet experienced people in your industry, these connections can save you time and money. Their knowledge can help you eliminate mistakes that may not be visible because of your own lack of experience. Other than reading books, networking with experienced entrepreneurs is the best way to avoid potential roadblocks and setbacks. Networking can also offer chances to take advantage of unforeseen opportunities. I can't stress the importance of networking with contractors enough. Although you may sometimes like to think you are offering a revolutionary product or service, the majority of the time, you are providing something already on the market. This is not a bad thing because it shows you that there is a demand for your product. You are just proving that you are capable of supplying what the consumer wants. The key is to always strive to provide a product that is superior in comparison to your competitors. There is room for more than one product in the same market; just make sure that the competition pales in comparison to what you have to offer. The wider your network becomes, the more knowledge you can obtain to help you in this area.

When I initially approached my lawyer about becoming my mentor, he assured me that he'd contact me once he ran across something that could help my business. I appreciated this because he didn't just spit out irrelevant information to seem knowledgeable. Be careful about choosing a mentor that is power-hungry or motivated by control. My mentor was being selective with his words; I could sense he only wanted to provide me beneficial advice. Eventually, he reached out and offered me the opportunity to network with another of his business clients. We were both in the fashion industry, but our target markets were different. I met with this business owner and we shared stories about how we started our companies. We discussed the joys and difficulties of being business owners. We also spoke about operational components such as marketing and distribution. It was a very humbling and inspirational meeting. We each left the meeting with additional knowledge that could benefit our individual businesses. This was the power of networking. My mentor had the insight to recognize how two of his clients had the potential to help each other in some fashion. He willingly opened his network to me, and it instantly paid dividends. Because we both agreed to stay in touch and support one another along our business journeys, my mentor was instrumental in helping me to expand my network.

Lastly, a good business mentor will be there to encourage and reassure you in times of doubt or need. Encouragement may be one of the most underrated characteristics of a good mentor. This may also be applicable for a spouse, friend or family member. With so much negativity in the world, surrounding yourself with people who offer words of encouragement at the right time is priceless. A good mentor, hopefully, has overcome similar difficulties and can provide you with reinforcement related to your current situation. It doesn't have to always be expert-level advice but just a few words of encouragement to keep moving forward. Of course, to be successful in life, we must be intrinsically motivated, but there are times when encouragement from others provides us with much-needed boosts of morale. When I became a business coach, one of my first realizations was the precious opportunity I possessed to encourage clients. Occasionally, as business owners, things may appear to be overwhelming; this usually is the point when you are on the brink of real success. You may be right at the cusp of your breakthrough. During these times, you can benefit from the experience of someone who has previously been in your shoes and recognizes exactly where you are spiritually, mentally and emotionally. An effective mentor will be there to encourage you and occasionally provide you with testimonies of victory in similar situations. It's often not a grand or illuminating conversation we need, but just a little encouragement from someone we admire and respect. Your mentor should be capable and willing to provide that encouragement on every occasion.

CHAPTER 21
How to find a Mentor?

You now know some valuable benefits of having a good mentor. As business owners and entrepreneurs, we all should take advantage of those benefits. It seems we live in an era where it has become popular for people to label themselves leaders and mentors. Good leaders and mentors are needed more than ever on both a personal and business level. We have all heard stories of reputable companies that were destroyed by poor leadership. Some of these companies provided great products and services for long periods of time. Some were even iconic in the business world. However, terrible business decisions made by their leaders completely overshadowed all the good they had previously done. Great leaders understand the importance of keeping quality counselors and mentors.

So, how do you find a good mentor? As in all relationships, in order to find something good, you must know what good looks like. A good mentor should be someone who challenges you to reach your full potential. The right mentor wants to see you prosper, so they are fully aware they must never let you become content with mediocrity. This may not be true of family or friends who may not want to ruffle your feathers. Being a friend is not the main responsibility of a good business mentor. The responsibility is to other aspects of your development, such as helping you develop the skills and attitude needed to become successful. They are responsible for helping you remain focused and disciplined throughout your business journey. That being said, sometimes they will need to show you tough love. You may not always enjoy that type of counsel, but it's a little easier to accept tough love when you know your mentor has your best interest at heart. A good mentor will not be afraid to ask you tough questions. Having the ability and fortitude to ask tough questions is one of the major qualities of a great mentor. Most new entrepreneurs are understandingly very optimistic and eager in the beginning stages of a new business journey. It's true that passion and optimism are needed to succeed in the business arena. Other characteristics, such as patience and effective strategizing are also needed. This is where a good mentor can really benefit you. They can also help you establish a solid foundation. This can be accomplished by asking questions that reveal the less visible behind-the-scenes work required to be successful. A lot of people like to listen to motivational and inspirational speeches, but they don't like to do the work required to be successful. Operating a successful business that serves others is a complete joy and honor, but it requires rolling up your sleeves and putting in grueling hours of extremely hard work. A good mentor will hold you accountable, by asking the appropriate questions to make you self-reflect and tackle important tasks that will lead to longevity.

Interestingly, you never know just where you may find a great mentor. You may discover your mentor online or it could be a neighboring business owner. Your mentor may come by referral from another business owner, family member or friend. Don't be afraid to search outside your normal environment to find a mentor. Knowing what a good mentor looks like will allow you to recognize them no matter the environment. Once you do find the right business mentor, the value of your business immediately has the potential to increase by leaps and bounds.

CHAPTER 22
Legacy of Service

One of the definitions for legacy reads: "Something transmitted by or received from an ancestor or predecessor or from the past." Leaving behind a good legacy is an intentional way to leave behind something valuable for your family and the world. Your legacy may include money, but contrary to popular belief, it's not just monetary. When it's my time to depart this earth, there are a few things I intend to leave behind. I'm grateful for the opportunity to start a business and become an author. Owning my passion has allowed me to intentionally build a legacy that will benefit others long after I'm physically gone. In Steven Covey's book, "The 7 Habits of Highly Effective People," he discusses the concept of beginning with the end in mind. This is simply suggesting that you should start off visualizing the finished product in the beginning. As a business owner, you should visualize your business helping others long after you're gone. You also should make sure the mission and values of your business are directly aligned with the type of legacy you wish to leave. Successful business owners have an opportunity to impact a mass group of people. You should strategically focus on using your business ventures to leave a noble legacy that will inspire others to serve. In order to leave a good legacy, you need to discover your most important principles and values. I will list some of the principles and values I want to be a part of my legacy.

With this text's focus catered towards business owners, I will discuss these principles and values in relation to entrepreneurship. However, they can apply to all of us on a personal level. First, I would like to use my business to leave a legacy of service. My first service is to God, which is why I take every opportunity to share my testimony with my clients whenever possible. My business was initially started on a prayer and deep passion for business. God answered that prayer for me years ago. I can truly say I'm living out a dream. So, every chance I get, His name will be deservingly glorified. Yes, I have earned a business degree, I've obtained business certifications, I've read countless business books, but none of my accomplishments would be possible without the power of God. He literally lifted me up and gave me the opportunity to operate my business with an amazingly powerful purpose.

Another way I'm able to leave a legacy of service is by consistently providing quality service to my clients. This is a tremendous opportunity for all entrepreneurs. I don't take for granted the trust my clients have in my experience and expertise. My goal is to do everything in my power to help each client understand and complete a thorough business plan. That's part of the reason I'm always looking to increase my skill level as a business coach. The more I invest into myself, the more value I can provide to my clients. That's why I'm a firm believer of the growth mindset. I want to give my clients more in value than I receive in money. I feel so much gratification when my clients are satisfied with my coaching services because customers always come first. Properly servicing customers is a core value of my business. A service attitude is great for business. If someone wants to prosper financially, all they have to do is consistently fill a need for a lot of people. Customers will not only seek you out for themselves but will also gladly refer other customers to you as well. Providing quality service to customers provides unlimited benefits in the short term and long run.

CHAPTER 23
Legacy of Courage

Next, I intend to leave a legacy of courage. When I first decided to become a legitimate business owner, it was just a vision. At that point, I realized nobody understood or believed in that vision but me. That's the harsh reality entrepreneurs may face in the beginning stages; there is no guarantee that a new business will succeed. Starting a business is a huge risk. The statistics for failing startup business are daunting. However, there are legitimate things you can do to minimize the risk of failure. First, you can create an excellent product or service that people truly want or need. Then, you should create a thorough business plan and use it as a roadmap and growth tool. Both steps mentioned are extremely valuable, but they still don't guarantee success. As an entrepreneur, you will be required to invest a lot of your time and energy. This is especially true in the beginning stages. There may be times when you are criticized heavily by insiders and outsiders. Without a doubt, there will be times when you absolutely feel like giving up and throwing in the towel. The lack of capital may become an issue early on. These are all legitimate and reasonable concerns when pursuing entrepreneurship.

However, if you're reading this book, chances are that you are prepared to move forward despite the risk involved with becoming an entrepreneur. You have something inside of you called courage that allows you to move forward amid fear.

Your reason for becoming an entrepreneur is stronger that any temporary setback that may occur. Even if you make a mistake or fail in the beginning, you will continue to learn and grow. This courage will allow you to accept constructive criticism from your clients so that you may create better products and services. You recognize that all the great entrepreneurs possessed this trait. Courage is a vital characteristic that is required for successful entrepreneurs. Business owners may differ in personality and strategy, but successful entrepreneurs recognize that they all must possess courage to be successful. This mindset can be developed over time as you continue to move forward. Performing small courageous acts every day will help you exercise and strengthen your courage muscle. Be courageous and remember that creating and operating a successful business is not for the faint of heart. Fortunately, you already possess inside of you all that you need to be successful.

CHAPTER 24
Legacy of Prosperity

Becoming prosperous by creating something that benefits others is an amazing opportunity. If you create wealth the right way, when you pass it down to your family, it becomes a blessing. With all the problems we face in this country, the United States still provides the best opportunity to create wealth through entrepreneurship. Creating a successful business may allow you the opportunity to leave an inheritance for generations to come. This may not be possible through working traditional 9-to-5 employments. Therefore, if you have an opportunity to start a business doing something you love, take full advantage of it. It would almost be selfish not to, when you know you can leave behind a legacy of prosperity for your family.

One of the definitions of prosperity is "to become strong and flourishing." I grew up in an area that has its share of poverty and violence. However, it is an area where some African-Americans have experienced great entrepreneurial success. Whether it be barbershops or restaurants, there are a few family names that conjure up images of success when mentioned. What do these families have in common with each other? They all were families successful at entrepreneurship. That spirit of success typically followed every child born of that family. The unique aspect of lasting success is it only takes one individual to get the ball rolling. The thought of your posterity inheriting a strong legacy, all because you had the vision and courage to become a business owner, should excite you. Whether my children decide to follow my footsteps of business ownership or not, I am committed to leaving a legacy of wealth and success.

Showing my children and loved ones that it is possible to create a successful business from scratch that produces lasting wealth is a wonderful privilege. Creating a fundamentally sound business built on hard work, service and excellence can change the course of your family history. It will raise the bar in a positive way for future family expectations. It is amazing how one person's success can change and enhance the identity of an entire family. When I speak of prosperity, it is not just acquiring material things, but also the mind state of settling for nothing less than success in all you do. So, never focus solely on immediate success, but envision your business being part of a legacy that lasts and represents prosperity.

CHAPTER 25
What Could Happen If You Don't Own Your Passion?

Is the thing you're passionate about related to a skill you have, that you wish to develop, and that's needed in the market? If the answer is "yes," then it's time for you to courageously push past all fear and reach your God-given potential. It's time for you to start that business you've been putting off for so long. If you have already established a business, then it's time to take it to the next level. Taking your business to the next level may mean better serving your customers or providing an improved product. The time is now for you to "own your passion." There comes a time in our lives, when the stars align for us in a good way. They may not align perfectly, but your vision will appear clearer than ever. During this time, it seems that divine favor is on your side. Spiritual people like to refer to this as "being in your season." When this time arrives, you must count it as a blessing and act immediately. This is your opportunity to share your God-given ability and talent with the world. This will allow you to serve other people and contribute to making the world a better place using your business as a vehicle. You were born for this particular moment and opportunity. Remember, to "own your passion" doesn't mean that you will not have to work, and that fear will not be present. There will be adversities and occasional doubts along the journey. Keep in mind that becoming a successful business owner requires a lot of hard work and courage.

However, the silver lining is knowing that owning your passion means you serve others doing work that you are truly passionate about. That's a win/win for everyone. I'm a business coach who loves teaching others how to build successful businesses. Who wins in this instance? My clients win because they are getting a coach who is passionate and dedicated to his craft. My business wins because the more customers I serve effectively, the more the business will grow.

My family wins because a successful business built on integrity will provide wealth, freedom, and a lasting legacy. Most importantly, regarding the success of my business, God will get the glory because I will always acknowledge that He is the one that blessed me with the divine ability to produce wealth. You may be an aspiring business owner who has been paralyzed by fear or procrastination. You may be a new business owner who is starting to feel overwhelmed and are close to giving up. Continue to focus on completing the next required action that moves you closer to fulfilling your dream. Just keep moving forward and gaining momentum. Again, entrepreneurship is not for everyone, but if you're reading this book, chances are that it's for you. There is a reason this book sparked your interest. You probably have a burning desire to build a prosperous business doing something you love. You are probably tired of living from paycheck to paycheck. More importantly, there may be something inside of you that seems to be unfulfilled.

Picture yourself 15-20 years from now. You're sitting at a restaurant waiting on your meal. It's Friday, and you're happy that the weekend is here because you've had a very challenging week. The long week stems from a bad conversation you had with your manager about your recent performance. Your manager feels that you've been underperforming. You feel that your manager doesn't really care about you and is only concerned with how your performance affects his future. There also has been a lot of tension at home with your family over a variety of issues. Even though no one has admitted it, you believe most of the issues are financially rooted.

The waitress brings out your food, and a couple of things immediately stand out about her. She's smiling uncontrollably and seems to be genuinely happy about life. Perhaps she is trying to provide excellent service so that she may receive a hefty tip. While that may be partly true, you sense a deeper source of her joyful behavior. You glance across the table and notice four guys in their later 20's or early 30's being seated. They are dressed casually, and everyone is smiling and appears to be very confident. As the waitress finishes serving your food, she acknowledges the guys at the table. She yells out, "Hey guys, good to see you. I will be over there in a second."

She goes over to them, and they all congratulate her on her upcoming business venture. They wish her luck and mention that they would like to work with her in the future. She responds saying she would love to work with them too and accepts one of their business cards. She admits to them that she was hoping they would return to the restaurant soon, because she had been so excited to share her good news. She takes their order and walks back to the kitchen. You can't wait for her to return to your table, so that you too can congratulate her. You are also curious to know who the men are sitting at the other table. The waitress checks in with you to see if you're satisfied with the food. You tell her you overheard the conversation she had with the gentleman at the other table. You congratulate her, and she beams with even more excitement. Then the excitement turns to tears - she apologizes to you for becoming emotional. She asks you if she can quickly share her story with you. She reveals that those guys at the other table have been coming to this restaurant for about 10 years. She explains that they always give her compliments about her leadership, prompt service and food expertise. About 5 years ago, she says they envisioned her owning a restaurant. They said her passion for food was evident and encouraged her to consider becoming a restaurant owner. The four men own one of the top business-consulting firms in the area. She said they started their business from scratch and were all millionaires. What stood out to her about them was their passion for business. She says they pop in about once a week and joyfully talk about anything business related. She goes on to tell you how she began to move towards becoming a restaurant owner about seven years prior. She admits that in the beginning, she didn't believe she had what it took to succeed as a business owner. She also says she was afraid that people would criticize her and fail to support her idea. She gave up about three times, but her passion for success, food, and freedom eventually conquered her fears. Although she still has moments of fear and trepidation, the joy of owning her business, based on something she truly loves, overrides her fear. She thanks you for allowing her to share her story.

Following that conversation, you begin to experience a number of mixed emotions. Part of you feels inspired by her testimony, but another part of you begins to feel a little sad. What no one in the restaurant knows is that you once possessed a strong desire to own your business, but you never moved forward with your ideas. Friends and colleagues always complimented you on your business expertise, but you let fear and distractions hinder you from acting on your desires. You walked into the restaurant feeling a little down, and now you're feeling worse than ever.

Even if you can unfortunately relate to this story, it's never too late to own your passion. Keep in mind, however, that some opportunities may eventually disappear without ever appearing again. You must seize the moment when the opportunity presents itself. So, if you're not currently a business owner, and you have the desire or calling to be one, you may be thinking, *where do I start?* A great starting point would be the question that was posed earlier. Is the thing that you're passionate about related to a skill you have, that you want to develop, and that's needed in the market? This question begins to break down the practicality of building a business that serves others. Next, proceed to develop a skill that complements your passion. For example, publicly speaking and writing complements my passion for building in an industry of business coaching. For me to continue to grow as a business coach, it would be wise for me to continue to improve in these areas.

Furthermore, the market indicated many new and existing business owners who needed business coaches. At that point, it was absolutely time for me to "own my passion." It was time for me to own it spiritually, mentally, emotionally and legally. It was time for me to provide quality services to those in need. Owning my passion has led to my launching a few different businesses that are all related in some aspect. Becoming a legitimate business owner has been a gift from God and I look forward to helping others do the same. Fear shows up in many different forms and intensity levels. Regardless of any fear or doubt, you must courageously move toward it and through it. You're reading this book for a reason, and more than likely, you possess a strong desire to become an entrepreneur. You must develop rock solid faith and perseverance. It will all be worth it in the end. If you are passionate about something that can benefit other people, please don't let anything stop you from moving forward. I strongly encourage you to pray and get with a business coach that can help you create a solid business plan. Owning your passion will bless you and your family for years to come. Your customers will be satisfied from the deliverance of a great product or service.

One of my key goals for this book is to inspire you to serve others doing something you truly love. In June of 2005, Steve Jobs delivered the now famous commencement speech to the graduates of Stanford University. After recently reading the transcript of the speech,

I felt enlightened and inspired. The speech was broken down into three simple stories. The first story was about connecting the dots. The second story was about love & loss. The third story was about death. As an aspiring business owner, how can these three stories help you?

First, let's explore how connecting the dots can help you along your business journey. In this speech, Steve Jobs stated, "You cannot connect the dots looking forward; you can only connect them looking backwards. So, you must trust that the dots will somehow connect in your future. You must trust in something - your gut, destiny, life, karma, whatever. This approach has never let me down, and it has made all the difference in my life." Personally, I can trust in my intuition and instinct because they are led by the wisdom of God. In the commencement speech, Steve Jobs spoke about "dropping out" and then "dropping in." He enrolled in college at the age of 17 and dropped out after six months. He discussed not really knowing what he wanted to do with his life, and he didn't really see how college would help him. On top of that, he was attending a very expensive school and didn't want to continue wasting his parents' hard-earned savings. So, he courageously dropped out, trusting that everything would work out in his favor. He admitted that dropping out was scary, but he acknowledged that it was one of the best decisions he ever made. After he dropped out, he was free from taking courses and studying fields he really had no passion to invest in or learn.

He talked about walking seven miles every Sunday night to get one good meal at the Hare Krishna Temple. It is compelling to read and learn about the struggles that successful people had to overcome. Too often, we latch onto the glitz and glamour portion of another's success and wonder why we don't receive similar results. When Steve Jobs used to walk to the temple, he noticed something that built up great curiosity inside him. A large portion of the world is still benefiting from this curiosity today.

At this time, nearby, Reed College was known for providing some of the finest calligraphy instruction in the country. One of the definitions of calligraphy, according to Webster dictionary is: "artistic, stylized, or elegant handwriting or lettering." Steve Jobs described how everything on the campus was beautifully done by a calligrapher. This is where the "dropping in" portion begins. Since he was free to take classes of his interest, he enrolled into a calligraphy class. At the time, he didn't know how this class would benefit him; he simply knew he had a passion for it. Many times, in life, God will nudge you to change direction without providing all the details. The direction may not be clear at the time, but your instinct tells you it's the right thing to do. Friends, family, and even you may not fully appreciate the complete vision at the time, but you must be courageous enough to follow and live in your truth even when it's not popular. Steve Jobs became fascinated by calligraphy. He later stated, "None of this even had a hope of any practical application in my life. But 10 years later, when we were designing the first Macintosh computer, it all came back to me. And we designed it all into the Mac. It was the first computer with beautiful typography. If I had never dropped in on that single course in college, the Mac would have never had multiple typefaces or proportionally-spaced fonts. And since Windows just copied the Mac, it's likely that no personal computer would have them. If I had never dropped out, I would have never dropped in on this calligraphy class, and personal computers might not have the wonderful typography that they do." We all know the impressive ending to this business story. Apple has grown to be one of the most innovative and groundbreaking business entities to grace the technological realm. Steve Jobs had the courage to initially follow his gut and build a business doing something he loved. He connected the dots. He had the desire and courage to "own his passion."

Looking back over your past, you will be able to see how specific experiences in your life happened for a reason. With the right outlook and mindset, you can see that being obedient to your inner voice will pay huge dividends in the long run. Not listening to your inner voice can be risky and regretful. Writing this book forced me to connect the dots in my own life. Again, I can recall engaging in my version of spring cleaning. I got rid of most of my old college books but just couldn't throw away that old college English book. Something in my gut told me that whatever future path I took, enhancing my writing skills would help me further my career. I carried that English book around in my backpack along with a writing tablet for years. During that time, I didn't know exactly where this studying would lead. I simply had the instinct to continue to sharpen the tool.

After practicing writing fundamentals and exercises from this book, I decided to pursue a writing certification. This led me to enroll in college to earn a second degree in English. I only took a couple of courses, but my confidence grew, and it helped to build and nurture a passion for writing about business. I promised myself that from that point on, my learning would consist only of classes, seminars, and books that fed and fulfilled an actual passion and purpose inside of me. Steve Jobs was curious about calligraphy. You may be curious about health & wellness, accounting, photography, fashion etc. Whatever the field, years from now, you will be able to connect the dots and see how it was instrumental in helping you reach your destination. Through prayer, meditation and patience, you will know that the urge is real and beneficial. The question becomes, will you be courageous enough to follow your truth? Will you be courageous enough to "own your passion?" When you are ready to answer "yes" to those questions, you will soon enough be able to take a retrospective look over your life and see how the pain, joy, successes and failures all were purposefully working in your favor. Being a man of faith, scripture provides me with great understanding and wisdom. In the Bible, Romans 8:28 reads: "And we know that all things work together for good to them that love God, to them who are called according to his purpose."

CHAPTER 26
Lose to Gain

Sometimes you have to hit rock bottom before you can spread your wings and fly. It's crazy to think that Steve Jobs was fired from Apple, the company he built from the ground up with Steve Wozniak. This had to be completely devastating and embarrassing for a talented visionary such as himself. He later stated, "I didn't see it then, but it turned out that getting fired from Apple was the best thing that could have ever happened to me. The heaviness of being successful was replaced by the lightness of being a beginner again, less sure about everything. It freed me to enter one of the most creative periods of my life." Sometimes we must symbolically, or literally, lose everything to gain it all. We all will eventually have an opportunity to share with the world our personal stories of love and loss. But, will we develop the courage and urgency to share it with the world? Ever since I was young, I carried a deep love for entrepreneurship. However, the love almost never manifested.

Years ago, I entered a period in my life that was somewhat deceiving. On the outside, I was prospering. I had been promoted to supervisor at a large company and oversaw leading a team of salespeople. In this leadership role, I was responsible for developing and implementing training programs for the new hires. I even received a management-training award that was somewhat unexpected. I had just moved into a decent suburban area in Metro Detroit. Being a single man and moving up the corporate ladder - some would view that period of my life as pretty good for me. It turned out to be what they call "fool's gold." What I didn't realize was that the bottom was about to fall out, and I would enter a very dark phase in my life. About nine months later, I was no longer employed with that company. The insurance department I worked in shut down business and moved to another state. I ran into huge financial distress, which was completely devastating. All the things that I had previously accumulated seemed to disappear or were in jeopardy of being taken away. It was by far one of the lowest points in my life. You talk about being humbled - this was definitely a "sink or swim" situation for me. I, admit, I even questioned God for the first time in my life. I recall being in my kitchen and saying, "God I know you're not about to let me go out like this." In hindsight, I now ask myself, who am I to question God? I proceeded to shed a couple of tears, and then I heard an inner voice say to me, "Get up." My life would never be the same again. As church people would say, there is no testimony without a test. I recall feeling a sense of peace come over me at that moment. It was a calm that I still can't explain. My financial situation was in shambles, but I truly felt that everything would be okay. It didn't seem like I had much help, but I still felt everything would be okay. I remember walking to the local Panera Bread with my laptop. I felt the urge to enroll into Christian ministry school. I had always appreciated and respected God's Word, but at this point, there was a deep hunger to strengthen my relationship with God. I began to desire a complete transformation and not just a temporary fix. It would be nice to say that outwardly things began to improve at this point, but that wouldn't be the truth. Although I felt a sense of peace about my predicament, some of my worst fears began to come true. I eventually lost a lot of things I had previously accumulated.

This loss turned out to be the best thing that could have happened to me. It forced me to really take a sincere look deep within myself and focus on becoming a better person. It forced me to honestly evaluate everything in me and around me. I started to seek wisdom and introspection about what really made me tick. In other words, I began to focus on strengthening my character and living out my purpose. Two things that continued to resonate in my heart were the desire to teach God's Word and the fervor for becoming a successful entrepreneur. Through the grace of God, I can say my passion for both is being manifested and currently on full display. During my hardship, I truly came to understand the real me. This clarity helped me to develop a high level of faith and patience. It also forced me to get creative, realizing that working for someone else would never truly satisfy me. No corporation could offer me the perfect position because there was no perfect position for me in Corporate America. I now understand that I was created and specifically designed to teach God's Word and to be an entrepreneur with a purpose. However, to walk in my calling, I had to go through the fire and become refined like a diamond. My dreams are now coming to fruition right before my eyes. I can look back and say that it was a blessing to fall because I got up stronger, wiser and more focused than ever. Being able to operate a business doing something I love gives me a sense of fulfillment. This would have never happened without the experience of those previous setbacks. Sometimes, you have to lose what you like in order to gain what you love.

CHAPTER 27
Death the Motivator?

Inspiration can be very elusive, so it's important to pay very close attention and take heed to whatever it is that inspires you. Strangely, one of the greatest sources of inspiration is the acceptance of death itself. How could death be a source of inspiration? One of the benefits of accepting the inevitability of death is that it can and should provide you with a sense of urgency. It also should help you focus on the truly important aspects of life. In the third story of Steve Jobs' Stanford speech, he stated, "Your time is limited, so don't waste it living someone else's life. And most important, have the courage to follow your heart and intuition." It's not the fear of failure that mentally paralyzes most of us, but rather the fear of negative criticism. Too often, our self-worth is tied to the thoughts and opinions of others. So many gifted individuals never fulfill their potential because they fear criticism from people who will never have their best interest at heart.

In a recent article, consultant Scott Hansen referenced the disturbing result of a survey from a popular magazine concerning death and funerals. It stated, "When you die, on average, the amount of people that will cry at your funeral is 10, and the number one factor whether or not people will come to your burial is based on the weather. If it rains, only ⅓ of the people that were scheduled to go will actually show up." If this survey is even close to being accurate, it should be even more unacceptable to allow the negativity of others halt you from achieving what God created you to do. Time waits for nobody. Many of our real heroes have passed away. Some of these heroes were individuals who seemed invincible to us as children. These individuals may consist of well-known social activists, spiritual leaders, great business leaders, mentors, family members and close friends. Death is something we all must face, but its imminence is also something that can be used as a tool to live a more fulfilling life.

I was taking my son to basketball practice recently, and we engaged in a deep conversation about courage. We began to discuss the importance of being courageous in the midst of fear. I shared with him that there had to be some level of fear for a person to display courage. Some may say they know those who never fear anything. The majority of the time, this is a facade because we all fear something. It is healthy to feel some level of fear about new and unfamiliar circumstances. So, I offered him advice that I hope will prove helpful for him long after I'm gone from this world. He began to listen closely, and I could sense that I really had his attention. As parents, we have the gift to accurately learn and interpret our kids' mannerisms. He looked at me with that gaze in his eye that symbolizes a student interested in the topic at hand. I looked him in his eye and said, "Son, every time you feel a spirit of fear, it's usually an opportunity to be courageous." It's amazing how a slight change in perception can free us from situations that previously kept us in bondage. This also includes the way we view death. As we continued our journey, I explained to him that I know one day, he and my other children may surround me on my deathbed if that's God's will. I said to him, "At that time, I don't want to regret not doing anything that I'm capable of doing right now."

This is my aim, whether it includes accepting Jesus as my Lord & Savior, forgiving others, spending more time with family, or starting my own business. I revealed to him how this visualization of my last days helps me to value the present, focus on priorities and live a more courageous life. Right now, you may be nervous about starting your own business or taking it to the next level.

Don't hesitate to use death as a tool by beginning with the end in mind. Life on earth is precious and short. Crush your fears with the tools of perspective and courage. Hopefully, you have identified your passion, and thoughtfully designed ways to use that passion to serve others. With the right team and mindset, you are prepared to own your passion. As the Chinese proverb states, "The journey of a thousand miles begins with one step." For you that were called to be successful entrepreneurs of integrity, act today and reap the benefits for a long time to come. There is no more time left to waste. Tomorrow is not promised. Today is the perfect time to "Own Your Passion."

www.ingramcontent.com/pod-product-compliance
Lightning Source LLC
Chambersburg PA
CBHW060616200326
41521CB00007B/789